Contents

Introduction

Poems nearer to the here and the now; poems of this years spring, summer, and autumn.

Days away, and longer vacations, including a return to the island, where much of my poetry began.

And maybe occasionally longer poems, for the notebook, where the poems first came to life, is indeed bigger than those of the past.

Poems also written on the hoof, and in the dead of night.

I hope there is not an overwhelming load of complaining, but I have suffered, with my frozen shoulder, through most of the time of writing.

I hope you are able to find something that brings a smile to your eye.

Christopher

November 2017

BBB Poem 1

Air lifted
Onto the pitch of global warming
We are gifted endless summer days
In springtime, in autumn
And no doubt, also in mid-winter

BBB Poem 2

I sweat, out of some frustration
The drawings don't make any sense
Yet I feel that scalp point sensation
Other woods, it seems they are less dense

The pencil is not driven, least ways
Not across the sketching paper plane
Instead I am distracted, same as ever was
The forms, the lines, the oddly triangular frame

My curves are corrupted, repetition
Cannot be repeated, seated here
By the windswept window, definition
Of lines now less well defined

And she reads the tea-leaves, says
All is well that is well, yet, yes yet
Not everything can be explained
The rain, though transitory, is near on to blame

BBB Poem 3

In that space, for those few moments
First watching
And then taking a photograph
Of the wren, stood contemplating
In the middle of the River Calder
In point of fact
Stood at the foot of a short waterfall
As viewed from a window
In the Hepworth Museum

So that short time, amplified many fold
Through these words, also by time backwards
To teenage years and just beyond
To bier-kellars, theatre clubs
Rugby league teams
And that first tax disc
On the day you passed your driving test
Going so so slowly back home
In the pea-soup of a fog

The queue behind you that day
Now dispersed
That is what you might imagine
As you mirror
Your own adventures over these fifty years
Half a century then
Of memories to call upon
As you frame, and focus on the heron
In the slip of water, on the River Calder

BBB Poem 4

And so, as you feel that warmth
Of peace, and love, and understanding
You feel that warmth, as you read your book
Whilst listening to your music

And so, as you feel that inner glow
Of care, of sharing, of being there
You feel that glow, in your imagination
Letting your thoughts wander as they wish

And so, as you remember to plan
For the future, with leanings from the past
As you feel for memories; the most recent
Also for the ones, from way further back in time

I know that the patience to draw is not here yet
Nor the desire, to take out the water colour set
Yet in the frame; I am not anywhere near ready
To trade a condemned artist's contemplations

I know that the swirls, and the shapes
The lines, and the escapes all add up
Yes, to draw the cup would be a pleasure
And o, to learn the potter's skill, what treasure

Yes, I know that I have built many barriers
And that breaking through is equally as tricky
As would be the heartbreak of letting go
And so I mow the lawn, trim trees, as best I can

BBB Poem 5

I take my mind with me, everywhere I go
My mind is my favourite friend
A friend I feel that I've grown to know

Years and years of memories
Are kept there
Kept in several stores

Reminders of those, at first
Closed, but now
Fully opened doors

It is the randomness
Which most appeals to me
Thoughts which arise

For all manner of reasons
Yes, whether it be on the hillside
Or down there, beside the sea

It is the absolute
Uncertainty, which pervades
Through all of the seasons

BBB Poem 6

A slow, soul fulfilling Saturday morning
Listening to Patsy Cline and Willie Nelson
Looking at photographs
From downalong, and backalong
Daydreaming of lullabies, and sacred moments
Waiting for the rush
Which when it comes, will still be a surprise
Such that I find references, from my past

On the windowsill
Photographs, paintings, and portraits
On the wall
A Rothko, reclaimed from a previous life
On the bookshelves
All of the poems, which cover up all of the loss

BBB Poem 7

The overnight rains were wilful

Pouring, and pouring, and pouring

But now, in the clear light of morning

The grasses are washed, the trees are washed

The garden is infected with new life

A blue sky is in the offing

And I am making tracks

To be with family, to be with art

BBB Poem 8

I know this place
Nearby is where I spent my formative years
I spot the base of Emley Moor Television mast
The remainder is shrouded in cloud, and mist
I remember the old mast
The winter of it being brought to ground
Due to the unbearable weight of ice, and snow

Those days, on the cusp of puberty
With girls just becoming a fascination
A few years though
Before my first broken heart
That is, a heart broken, by a girl
Not by my parents, or by my so called friends
Or by my Penistone Grammar school teachers

I left this place
But, like a bad penny, returned several times
Mostly in search of solace, or shelter
After further experiences
Of break-ups, and heartbreaks
Or after split-ups; moving-on proclamations
I am here today as a result of one such

Here today to go to an art gallery
Twenty five or more miles away
Salts Mill; the home of one David Hockney
Another Yorkshireman, yet such a soul
Who travelled way further than I did
And who picked up, quite rightly
Many more plaudits along the way

BBB Poem 9

Wounds have little choice but to be transitory
Yet it takes a good half, of a dull wet morning
For me even to reach into the emptiness of
The nothingness which only existed fleetingly

Although a door was opening; the half silence
And the half-tired mindless daydreaming
Led me to that place of feeling, feeling though
Not of rational self, not of this conscious self

As if ones mind (brain) had been opened
By a tin opener, for it to breathe in the many
Airs; of irresponsibility, hope, and anguish
With the canopy lifted, my thoughts could fly

BBB Poem 10

Sat, in the garden of mindfulness
At *Doddington Hall*
There are fountains
But also people talking loudly
As though they are mindful
Of their need to be heard
The gardener meanwhile
Respects the peace, he works
The soil relatively quietly
With his hoe, with his rake

One noisy woman
Is replaced by another, this time
A specie with gesticulation
And loosely flailing arms
The fountain, god bless the fountain
Masks the worst of her utterances
At last I am alone, with only the feint sound
Of children at play in the distance for company

If I knew the names of flowers I would tell you
The reds, the pinks, the whites
There are crimsons, yellows, and blues
And of course all nestled
In green foliage; green grass, green leaves
Green stalks, and green shoots
Thee is also a poppy, or two
Behind the big house and the rose garden

At ten-past-twelve or so, in the corner, a tree
At ten-to-twelve or so, a house, and a gate

The sky is grey, filled with cloud, yet I believe
Little threat of rain; it is warm, comfortable
With only the merest hint of birdsong

BBB Poem 11

You cannot be with me today
And that is unfortunate
For the scented notes in the garden
I feel would be rather to your liking
As might the still water
In the restaurant, where I wait for lunch

The glass bottle
Has a fancy stopper contraption
Which, by my age, I ought to understand
How to operate; of course I do manage
Though you would not say
That mine was a dignified manoeuvre

You will not be with me tomorrow
Which vexes me
For we could have many opportunities
To take pleasure, and share enjoyment
Perhaps at the seaside
To take in the salt water's air

Or to find a burbling stream
Out on the moors
Where we could take off our shoes
And paddle, before we sated ourselves
With love making, followed
By lashings of strawberries and cream

BBB Poem 12

In that distance, which you talked about
Do you ever hope to find me
Yes I am there, I do wait, I often wait
Yet it tires me, the wait wears me out

In that nearness, when you touch me
Do you know how good I feel
Yes I am there, to love you, I often love you
Yet it needs me, love calls me out

That the distance, and the nearness
Conspire to keep you from me
Yes I am here, to wonder, I often wonder
Yet it feels me, wonder finds me out

In that time, which I dwell in
Do you care for where I am
Yes, I want to be, I do doubt, often I doubt
Yet it leaves me, care wears me out

In that space, which I frequent
Do you hear me ticking over
Yes I have to do so, I shake, often I shake
Yet it catches me, space calls me out

Thus the times, and the spaces
Are arranged to keep you from me
Yes I want to be, I often have to do so
Yet they wrangle, they do so find me out

BBB Poem 13

It is a blue sky Saturday morning
I could wear a white shirt, and denim jeans
I ought to walk alongside the harbour
And take a coffee, at the top of the slip

I should sit, and wait
I should sit, and be
And in between the waiting, and the being
I remember, that I am no longer with you

It is a sun filled Saturday morning
I could take a bath, have a shave
I ought to soak, perspire even
And make myself thoroughly pleasant

I should stroll, and sojourn
I should be the flaneur
And in between the bathing, and the strolling
I remember, that I am no longer with you

It is a bright light Saturday morning
I could lay your clothes out
I ought to layer your silks
And use the mirror to choose the colours

I should skip, and laugh
I should smile with joy
And in between the joy, and the laughter
I remember, that I am no longer with you

BBB Poem 14

I didn't take breakfast at the breakwater
I came here
Because you may have wanted me to
Though I have no memory
Of St Catherine, or of being here with you

Move on

To Rozel Bay
Where *Beau Couperon* hotel as was
Is now a ten million pounds private dwelling
With its own steps onto the beach
From the door in the battlement wall

I came here
Because we stayed in the one-time hotel
Which is now someone's house
I remember a balcony, a shingle beach
I remember rock-pools, a meal in the restaurant

Wasn't it the year we went to St Malo
Also to Samares Manor
I know these facts
Because of the photographs, stored digitally
On many computers, since those very days

Move on

To Archirondel, and the *Driftwood Cafe*
Where I have ordered breakfast
Taken snaps of sea, and rocks, and the tower

I don't recall sitting here with you
Yet I feel I must have

I imagine, that in ten years time, or so
This place
Will also have gone upmarket
In the style of *El Tico*, and *La Braye* at St Ouens
Altogether more gentrified than I remember

BBB Poem 15

Granite houses
Granite walls
Granite quarries
Granite souls

Soft sand beaches
Slowly turning surf
Hold on to your reaches
For what it is that I am worth

Granite towers
Granite stepped
Granite defences
Granite swept

Silver screen horizons
Fishermen's old boats
Prayers to Zion
Gathered with all my hopes

Granite outcrop
Granite coastline
Granite harbours
Granite moonshine

Waves turning, also lapping
Before the shingle boar
Sea breeze on faces mapping
Quiet now, the departing roar

BBB Poem 16

Where love was lost
Where lust was found
To touch-tone evenings
Is where we were bound

From Gorey to St Aubin
From restaurant to bar
To you being propositioned
Beneath the moonlit star

Where aches were shared
Where pains were hidden
To touch-tone evenings
Is where we were bidden

From airport to airport
From car to car
To our becoming lovers
Plans offered from afar

Where smiles were ours
Where frowns were left behind
To touch-tone evenings
Is where we were ultra-kind

From house to flat
From together to apart
To becoming parents
New dreams to start

Where tiredness did enter

Where impatience arose
Those touch-tone evenings
Brought silent, to a close

BBB Poem 17

Today it is Plemont
Last night was the Oyster Box
I tell you this for no reason
Other than for love, or is it for the paradox

Today it is rocks and cliffs
Last night; oysters in champagne butter sauce
I tell you this with naught held back
Other than for love, or is it for the vibrant rose

Today it is clouds and sands
Last night was lights along the promenade
I tell you this as if for anything
Other than for love, or for the Marquis de Sade

Today the rib is cancelled
Last night was the opera house
I tell you this with a care to record
Other than for love, or is it for the lousy louse

Today it is wind, and rain
Last night was Newton Faulkner's songs
I tell you this in case you see me
Other than for love, or the rights and wrongs

BBB Poem 18

It is easier for me to write
Than it is for me to sketch or paint
For one thing I am less certain
Of my mistakes, with the written word

Also I am able to go back in time
To many places; all at a once almost
And I can root around, to find my feelings
To gather in; my past, my present emotions

And as I attempt to convey what I feel
Of love, lust, longing, and loss
I myself share in, and enrich my imagination
With feelings, of love, lust, longing, and loss

The writer's world is left, right, back, and front
Above, and below
To the very extremes of perception
Writings of witnessing the vanishing horizon

Between land, and sky, and sea
Listening intently, and seriously engaged
By David Hockney, talking on the radio
About art, as I soaked in my moonlit bath

The certainty, that one word will follow another
A couple of words will be offered up to me
By a view, by music, by dance-steps, by a film
Of the seasons; meditations, an island in a lake

And, in contrast

By the doubt that the words will not be read
Or will not be understood
By the person, or by the audience

For whom they were aimed at
For whom, and without whom
They have no purpose
Neither in this life, nor in the next life

BBB Poem 19

I have not found you yet
But I have, believe me, been looking
No, I have not found you yet

I have surveyed the coasts and beaches
Where, believe me, I have been looking
Yes, I have surveyed the coasts and beaches

I have climbed towers and breakwaters
Where, believe me, I searched and searched
Yes, I have climbed towers and breakwaters

I have driven; north, south, east, and west
Where, believe me, I kept a keen lookout
Yes, I have driven; north, south, east, and west

I dined in beach cafes, and fine restaurants
Where, believe me, I may taste your presence
Yes, I dined in beach cafes, and fine restaurants

I shopped, in high streets, and market halls
Where, believe me, clothes you wore still hang
Yes, I shopped, in high streets, and market halls

I have set myself, to the sun, the wind, the rain
Where, believe me, I sensed skin, as your skin
Yes, I set myself, into the sun, the wind, the rain

I have not given up on you yet
Believe me, I have kept on saying that
No, I have not given up on you yet

BBB Poem 20

It was a winter's night
Or was it early spring
Either way it was dark
As we came out of the restaurant
Just up the hill from the floodlit castle

It wasn't the first time
That you had rebuffed me
But on this particular occasion
You had taken me out for a romantic meal
To break the news of closure

Repeatedly you reminded me
Of my responsibilities to my family
Repeatedly I reminded you
That that stretch of my life was behind me
That, for my souls sake, I had had to move on

You did not want to pull close to me
Outside under the street light
You did not want me to hold you
Not closely, not intimately
Not in any sort of public declaration

But I hung on in there
And we talked, on our return drive
Five miles or more, along the coast road
You took me into your house, upstairs
Into your lounge, there to sleep on your floor

BBB Poem 21

The boats could be in St Ives
But no, they are not
The sky, and the sea, could be blue, and azure
But no, they are cloud grey, and murky taupe

The hotel could be in St Mawes
But no, it is not
The bedrooms could be five star boutique
But no, they are net curtained, dormer windows

The castle could be Warwick, or Carcassonne
But no, certainly not
Dining could be a gastronomic adventure
But no, it is cold pie, in the bus shelter

The shops could be arts, and crafts, and unique
But no, no, not at all
Buying gifts could be a pleasure of celebration
But no, it is pearl, or pearl, or pearl

The writing could be gentle, and purposeful
But no, most definitely not
The words could be observational, and sincere
But no, today it is sarcasm, that rules the roost

BBB Poem 22

Sands, firm wet sands
A brave red sunrise
Sands, soft dry sands
A wild red sunset

You
Brave, and red
You
Wild, and wet

Restaurant, de-luxe
Patrons, chic, classy
Restaurant, Michelin star
Patrons, beautiful bodies

You
Chic, classy
You
Beautiful body

Fashions, haute-couture
Tight, clinging
Fashions, fabricated gold
Loose, swirling

You
Haute-couture
You
Tight, swirling

BBB Poem 23

The rains came
I was asked to move my bag
The man, who had made the request
Sat down and consulted his mobile phone
And said
Michael's not up to it
Malcom's not up to it
The woman, who could be the wife
Had also sat down
She says to say that they will be back by four
I take a photograph, to capture the rain
I am reminded of a song
But do not go there
A number 2 bus arrives, and departs
A lady with a blue check umbrella walks by
Vowing not to go in any more shops
Yet I notice
She heads straight for the souvenir emporium
Whose neon sign states that yes, they are open
We might have a pizza tonight
In a restaurant without a licence
Though I have to be honest and say
That I have yet to see this particular establishment
Nor have I witnessed the likes of its clientele

BBB Poem 24

So, for two days we have had rain
And for eight days, we have had sun
Even today, on one of the rain days
The day began with sunshine and blue sky

One could become dispirited
By the overflowing gutters
By the mist enveloping the bay
One could, but simply by the law of averages

One can be certain that the sun will return
That the spirits will be lifted
By the clearer skies, by the lapping
Of the azure sea, onto the silver sunlit sands

Is this what Beckett was aiming at
With Godot; that to wait is the life
To wait, and to observe, no more to it than that
No need for despondency, nor for hope

Of course if the rain has set itself in
Which by now it seems to have done
Then, I agree, one may well struggle
To visualise any emerging light

BBB Poem 25

I'm through with looking for you
So now I am leaving
I'm through with looking for you
From now on I am disbelieving
I'm through with looking for you
No more is this old man grieving

I went to the Battle of Flowers
Watched floats go this way and that
The parishes had gathered their powers
To put on their extravagant top hat
Everyone was supposed to be there
But I saw no sign of you, no sign of you

I'm through with looking for you
So now I am leaving
I'm through with looking for you
From now on I am disbelieving
I'm through with looking for you
No more is this old man grieving

I took so so many photographs
I even videoed the larger players
So so many people joining in
To make the day a festive affair
Everyone was supposed to be there
But I saw no sign of you, no sign of you

I'm through with looking for you
So now I am leaving
I'm through with looking for you

From now on I am disbelieving
I'm through with looking for you
No more is this old man grieving

Later, in the editing suite
I searched for you once again
All through those half-smile glances
Which failed to raise my disdain
Everyone was supposed to be there
But I saw no sign of you, no sign of you

I'm through with looking for you
So now I am leaving
I'm through with looking for you
From now on I am disbelieving
I'm through with looking for you
No more is this old man grieving

I won't be back next year
Unless of course things change
I will stop my self-berating
And move on down the range
Everyone was supposed to be there
But I saw no sign of you, no sign of you

I'm through with looking for you
So now I am leaving
I'm through with looking for you
From now on I am disbelieving
I'm through with looking for you
No more is this old man grieving

BBB Poem 26

I thought I could not explain
But now I think I can
Yes, now I think I can
I went there in search of the duende
For I had found the duende there
Once upon a time before

The bookshop is no longer there
The restaurant is no longer there
The beach hotel is no longer there
It is damned hard to search for the duende
When one searches alone
When one searches alone

The bedroom is no longer there
The bathroom is no longer there
The lover is no longer there
It is so so difficult to search for the duende
When one searches alone
When one searches alone

The imagery is no longer there
The feeling is no longer there
The transference is no longer there
It is surely impossible to search for the duende
When one searches alone
When one searches alone

I thought I could explain
But now I think I cannot
Yes, now I think I cannot

I went there in search of the duende
For I had found the duende there
Once upon a time before

BBB Poem 27

In this time
In this time of physical pain
In this time of physical pain
And mentally prepared dullness

The union flag waves
The union flag waves as the sunlight streams
The union flag waves
As the sunlight streams through windows

The blue sky
The blue sky with nary a cloud
The blue sky with nary a cloud
To cover the Lincolnshire Wolds

In this time
In this time of cushions on settees
In this time of cushions on settees
And a pot of tea on the table

The room is still
The room is still and once was quiet
The room is still and once was quiet
Quiet, and impeccably peaceful

The house
The house comes to life
The house comes to life
With the first sounds of the day

In this time

In this time of dew on the grass
In this time of dew on the grass
And birdsong in the garden

The writer writes
The writer writes to ease his pain
The writer writes to ease his pain
And thus begins his own mourning

The commentator looks on
The commentator looks on to the shadows cast
The commentator looks on to the shadows cast
And towards the long thoughts lost

BBB Poem 28

It is still a summer breeze
Even after our Channel Islands vacation
There are still leaves on the trees
Even after I surveyed the state
Of that small station

The pampas grass commands the views
Its circumference doubled
Thanks to sun and rain
I am listening to Nils Frahm
His album titled *Screws*

In my gentle meditation
I am thankful for the pain
The little yellow wheelbarrow
Does not know where to sit
The jet fighters manoeuvres

They rock the ground and the sky
Captain Corelli's Mandolin
Those houses that took a hit
The world's ammunition factories
O why, o why, o why

It is still a summer breeze
Beneath the mid-August daydream
There are apples, there are peaches to seize
There are thoughts, of love
Love on which to scheme

There are masses of blackberries

Although some still a youthful red
The garden eases, teases out my worries
Lets me write those missing words
Those words which I never ever said

The grass seeds, which I planted backalong
Have covered the bare and damaged ground
The thymes, the reed grass
All are coming on strong
The pianist, and the bass player, gift their song

BBB Poem 29

The marching band is present
So are the mowers of lawns
I could be in *Mornington Crescent*
Or where one sees the salmon spawns

Yet, from this quiet corner
I see the pile of garden waste
I am, as if the wayward mourner
Who left his past in clouds of haste

But I have the towering willow
And apple trees bearing fruit
My lovers head is on her pillow
And much the same I will follow suit

Not denying part, or all, of my creation
Not looking for ways in, nor ways out
It is my time alone, this nation
Where I ease away the seeds of doubt

BBB Poem 30

It is a tunnel
A telescope
A path across a vista

A route map for correspondence
And communication
Between lovers, and lovers of life

It is a train
An aeroplane
A ways, and a means

Of moving, from here, to there
And back again
For lovers, for lovers of life

It is a stream
A river
A never ending flow of cool water

From the source, to the sea
All around the cycle
As with lovers, as with lovers of life

BBB Poem 31

I go out into the garden
In the fresh morning air
But where has my zafu gone
I must have misplaced it

I feel the cooler breeze
Over my skin, under my linen shirt
I listen to the album *Atomos*
By Winged victory for the sullen

Are you searching for something
Which I do not give to you
Are you quietly saying to me
That we each have our own past lives

Are you leaning, as the plum tree leans
Towards the light, towards the sun
Towards the source of growth
Is it more growth which you crave

The concert hall in Los Angeles
Is not lost to me, although
The music that evening was not special
But I do have a CD to remind me

Of the visitation of angels, which was
A place, at that particular moment in time
Where I often lost myself, or where
I allowed my mind to wander in joy

My past is almost unapproachable now

I guess that is why I am still writing
That is why I sit out in the garden
To gather the splinters from a past life

BBB Poem 32

The love was too strong
It hid all the sufferances
The love went on too long
It followed the circumferences

Why would I write that
Why would I construct
Or record these utterances

Why would I want you to know
The chances that I'd taken
The hopes and the undulations

The love was too tough
It bid all the challenges
The love became too rough
It wallowed in the imbalances

Why would I write to you
Why would I deduct
Or inform the dalliances

Why would I share this
The images that were torn
As I stripped back the valances

The love was real
It undid all the differences
The love was to feel
To re-open the sufferances

BBB Poem 33

I bring my own sounds
To counteract the hammer, to overwhelm
The nails, the hedge trimmer, the rolling along
Of the waste collection bins

I bring *Bubbling Spring*
To enhance the jazz
Of suburban urban living
I ask focussed noise, to disperse random noise

And now the industrial scale
Garden vacuum machine is set to work
Picking up, or blowing away
All of the fallen foliage of the summer

Would that I could build
A super-strength sound insular summer house
Or an equally peaceful meditation chapel
O would that I could do so many things

For a moment there the breeze took hold
Ruffled the hair over my forehead
Cleared away a cloud; the light came through
Gave me my very own patch of peace

My daughter messaged; could she stay over
Bring my two grandchildren for the weekend
Before the bank holiday; if the weather is
Promising, maybe we could go to Cleethorpes!

BBB Poem 34

He did not mean to complain
In point of fact he did not complain
He simply made an accurate observation
However, his life was a life lived in pain
And so it was not unnatural
For his first thoughts to be thoughts of pain

In that idyll, in that peaceful village
His home, for many a year now
And hers too, for only a few years less
A togetherness of life, of a life lived together
Yet all the while his limitations limited
His adventures, his day by day adventures

The doctor called by, but now travels widely
His friend, and her partner, had called by
But they had not returned, not yet returned
Which he was sure they had promised to do
But of course they led very busy lives
With families, friends, and circles of society

He did not mean to sound bitter
In point of fact he did not sound bitter
He was matter of fact, straight to the point
However his life had minimal visitations
And so it was not at all surprising
For his first thoughts to be of a relaxant

With easement, in this place of inhaled calm
His passage, his journey was partly fulfilled
And hers too, to see him freed from suffering

This was, a thought out, measurement of life
A considered measurement, made together
Because always their minds remained creative

BBB Poem 35

I saw images
Call them visualisations if you will
Indescribable objectivity
Shrouded in mists
With several layers of substance, and shadows
A monochrome display
Yet with tone
Yes with lots of tones
Tones to set the spirits dancing
Tones to bring the meditation to life

A meditation on love
A meditation on breathing
A meditation on those most important words
I am here for you my love
Darling, I am here for you now
I was in the present moment
The suns heat warmed my painful shoulder
I was sat before the thriving plum tree
Which I had rescued a few winters past
Whose fruit was now coming to fruition

BBB Poem 36

The stillness of the early morning
As seen over the corner of the roof
Of next doors bungalow

It is still because it is early
It is early because I woke early
Not though to see the stillness

Nor particularly to listen to
Tallulah Bankhead, reading Dorothy
Parker's poem *Telephone Call*

O what a performance
O what a performance
O how early in the morning

Awake as the light broke
As the darkness gifted the day
As the day took over

And said to me
Look at the roses
Look at the garden, which is still

It is still, because that is how days do begin
Days begin that way because I wake early
I wake early because how else

To catch the stillness
To feel the stillness
To record the stillness

BBB Poem 37

It is you who keeps me warm
Not the loose words
Written of, or for, anyone other

It is you who saved me
From the eye of the storm
To become my real life true lover

It is you who I have to warn
I have somehow to be, to be
So pray, be light, do not smother

It is you who makes you torn
Better not to analyse so, instead
Let love help you, to rediscover

It is you who I wake by in the morn
You, who brought me to your bed
To watch, as slowly I did recover

It is you, whose doubts I duly scorn
Whose mind and body, when held firm
Gift the light, gift the leave to suffer

It is you, who waves to me with smiling eyes
You, with your once tearful eyes reformed
The love to build us up, the way to be tougher

BBB Poem 38

I look at thousands of images on Tumblr
        In the public realm
Then I find one of you, in my private collection
        The last one

I read hundreds of inspirational quotations
        Offered to all and everyone
Then I find a poem, written by you
        The final one for me

I listen to dozens of my own written words
        Recorded over time
Then I hear your voice, on a long boat; words
        Of mild chastisement

I have a book delivered, by a singular courier
        On this day of fine-rain showers
I decide that I will post one copy on to you
        Tagged: To Wendy, as a surprise

I am to take a bath, to soak, and meditate
        To contemplate upon my navel
I recall a bathroom, where together we shaved
        Here, there, and everywhere

BBB Poem 39

There is a fine drizzle
After several days of dry weather
The water butt is slowly filling
Following several days of emptiness

The grass is dampness over dew
And the petals gather droplets
The woodpile is also overcome
From tinder core, to surface damp

The cricket match carries on
Into the fifth day, at Headingley
The result is still in the balance, pray
A conclusion is reached before the rain

There was a fine drizzle in the North
After several days of neat Jersey weather
The night time bus stop was mine
After several hours on the darkened train

These thoughts are of lightness over blue
As the memories of old push on in
There is a family where I am going
There is a family where I have been

There is a big-game football match
This coming weekend, at Hillsborough
I will be welcomed back after my absence
Though no conclusion I fear is expected

BBB Poem 40

Are you the one who
Cries out for the heartache of love
Do you seek
The let's make up and move on of love

Is it you who
Fashioned the doubt and the despair of love
Do you truly
Desire the nay never a care of love

Can you not be the one
Who says back off, and beware of love
Are you the one who
Goes after the smouldering stares of love

Do you seek
To hear the screams, for the sake of love
Is it you who
Listens, longing for the soulful song of love

Do you truly
Inspire the dare, for the lingering kiss of love
Can you not be the one
Who holds the painful hit and miss of love

Are you the one who
Who is fearful of the diss, the distance of love
Do you seek
To tour the alps, to savour the swizz of love

BBB Poem 41

It is the day when I said I would start walking
Of course it is raining, but only a fine drizzle
Yet still sufficient to delay my departure

It is the fifth day of the cricket test match
Between England, and the West Indies
Much had been made before this game

About the poor state
Of West Indies cricket, some
Said terminal decline

Yet here, on the final day, they are
Still in with a chance
Albeit some say, a small chance

Seventeen minutes to go until lunch
Two hundred and fifty runs
Are needed for victory

Or eight wickets have to fall
Before defeat could be
Some say would be, confirmed

All around me
I have distractions
To save me from the walking

Yet it is the cricket commentary
Yes, TMS is the itch
Which I simply cannot foil to scratch

I ought to tell you
That I recently bought a cagoule
Especially for

Changeable weather such as this
I see it now staring out at me
From the chair back

The LBW shout is given not out
My new coat's shout
Is given not out

The Test Match Special team move on
To discuss ways of playing bridge
They too are also so so easily distracted

BBB Poem 42

Right now I am sat
In a chair, in a room
With nothing pressing to be done

What would it feel like
To sit in another chair, in another room
With nothing pressing to be done

I think of Buckfast Monastery
Sat in a bedside chair, in a visitors room
With nothing pressing to be done

Rapidly then I think
Of all of those chairs, in all of those rooms
With nothing pressing to be done

I wonder what it means, or feels like
To sit on a chair, in a room
With nothing pressing to be done

The pleasure of the sunlight streaming
As I sat, on a chair, in a room
With nothing pressing to be done

The restlessness, caused by the grey clouds
As I sat, on that same chair, in that same room
With nothing pressing to be done

Allowing the dullness of weather to affect me
As I sat, on a chair, in a room
With nothing pressing to be done

To see the red leaves, brightened by the rain
As I sit, on that chair, in that room
With nothing pressing to be done

BBB Poem 43

I feel altogether elemental
No, I know it's not the right word
But I have to claim something
Claim the erectness
Claim the fluidity of the moment
In stocking feet, gliding faultlessly
Over the wooden hallway floor
I am here, I am now, I am mindful
That to feel so good is a wonder
Which I ought to breathe in
Which I ought to breathe out
Time, and time, and time again
Of course there are rubbish bins to empty
Dishwashers to unload
New CD's to be loaded onto the computer
But hey ho
Already today I have watched Lachlan Goudie's
Awesome Beauty, The Art of Industrial Britain
Which both confirmed my love of nostalgia
As well as my belief in the future of youth
The future of humanity
Who have lived in, and still do live in
A life worth living

BBB Poem 44

First I felt the lack of light
As I stood at the stove cooking dinner
All the while listening to Craig Finn
Sing from his album
We all want the same things

Last night he saw something
Which he didn't see coming
But I can tell you, I knew that this night
The rains were on their way, and the deluge
The downpour did not in any way disappoint

The double glazed French doors
They took the brunt of it
Yet the advertisers feather would still float
The designers, the manufacturers, the installers
Should be proud; the weather was kept at bay

The torrential rain continues, sounds arise
From all sides of the house
And from the rooftops, where
The chimney pots are also getting battered
Yet, from my Harris Tweed vantage point

I can see a patch of silver-blue sky
Away out in the distance
I can see through the shear vertical raindrops
Yes, the Union flag hangs limp, lost on this day
But the blossom tree says;, I can handle this

Though that is before I see

The first streaks of lightning
Closely followed, by the thunder's rumble
The silver-blue sky smiles, as if about to say
Come to me now why don't you, I am waiting

I think of the passions
And the longings
I think to the desires
And those many other destructions
Long now gone

BBB Poem 45

The dew is on the grass
Yes I know, I am missing two syllables
But I am singing their song already

The sand is on the beach
Yes I know, that line is not even in there
However, the past is all I have to teach me

For don't you see, no now don't you
The light, so early
The light so surely transports you

For with a tune in the head
And a pot of tea in the hand
God damned youth I wished to kiss you again

Restrained, minimally, as I am
By being the only existentialist
In the room at the moment

If only the Everly Brothers
Had been around
Their sound might well have saved me

Bade me not to walk barefoot in the grass
Nor to pass up the chance
To dance the night away, dance the night away

Yet, all in all, the call has to be made
That it's been a good year for the roses
Highlighted by walking out in the morning dew

BBB Poem 46

I had no intention of jumping into the lake
Anyway it was winter
And I had just left the warmth of your bed
Ok, I had left it for the last time
So I was a little despondent
But me, jump in the lake, no, never

Of course I was sore
That you had asked me to leave
Yet, for the very first time
I saw the frost, in the hollow
On the fifth green of the golf course
But me, too sore, no, never

What is the point of continuing
If you have already made the point
But I will continue
I will reinforce the hurt, and the heartache
Of leaving you, in your warm bed
To think, what is the point of continuing

BBB Poem 47

Maxim is the real deal
I am the great pretender
He writes for a magazine
Makes covers; for books
For LP's, and CD cases

He is a renaissance man
Looking after the children
While his wife goes to work
Fiona, Maxim's wife
Is also the real deal

Soon she will have borne
Her fourth impressive child
Also, at our writing group
She continues to set
A most unique standard

Kate, my partner is the real deal too
She married Maxim and Fiona
By the river, outside Hubbards Hills
And again, this time in the park, where
The wedding couple arrived on a tandem

Kate is a renaissance woman
Once an NHS IT project manager
With little knowledge of IT
Now she is an humanist celebrant
Who knows lots about humanity

BBB Poem 48

The picture isn't especially good
In fact it edges towards pornographic
But doesn't quite make that either
The caption though, the caption lifts it
His hand is fumbling for her crotch
'Mine, he whispers'
'Yours, she breathes'
I have no choice but to save it
That is to write down this memory
Of how, for once
The words were worth a thousand pictures

BBB Poem 49

I expect many things
When you receive the book
But most of all, yes most of all
I expect the unexpected

For you to be surprised
By my surprise
Would be more than ok
Way more than ok

For you to be ambivalent
About the content
Well I could understand that
It's been a long time after all

But for you to be in denial
To return it without reading
(Which is what I do expect)
That might clear a few horizons

Though for you to take a care
To read the whole thing closely
Pointing out any mistakes
Would be a truly welcome outturn

And for you to be pulsed with joy
Your emotions openly rendered
To a time ever to be remembered
Then that I would love to know

For you to feel the love

Maybe even to share the love
As once I believe you did share love
For that a telegraph would suffice

BBB Poem 50

You reach for the unreachable
Yet are unable to haul the boat ashore
You turn to philosophy
To other men's observations
Yet you say that you are indifferent
To the indifference
It is only a superficial statement, nothing at all
To do with the reflections of love, of poetry

You would take off your shoes and socks
Roll up your cotton chino trousers
Stride out into the water, wilful
To haul the boat ashore
Yet the vessel is empty
She is in there no more
Nothing now but the defections
The deflections of love, and poetry

Instead you sip your cold coffee
Rock a little while, in your rocking chair
Nothing now is nothing, nor as it ever was

BBB Poem 51

It's time for a light meter check
As the videographer films inside the old boat
It's time for a nod, a shake of the head
A young man, tries
To keep his telephone love afloat

It's time for the race day final preparations
The riders are en-route, to be here by three
The commentators rehearsals are in full swing
He has an excitable voice
I look quietly out to sea

BBB Poem 52

The beachcombers are by the sculpture
Metal detectors in their hands
I walk across the pebbles to the sculpture
Not though to the sound of marching bands

It's what I've heard called a shingle beach
Where you have to walk n single file
It's not safe to be caught coyly holding hands
Rather *Plus-Fours* could be your chosen style

They'd have them in the gentleman's outfitters
And, to be honest, you'd look rather grand
What with the *Barbour*, and the *Burberry*
And the shooting stick with which to stand

BBB Poem 53

September in the sunshine
Breakfast in the bay
A pavement cafe actually
Beside a crying child's affray

Why not add a rack of sourdough toast
Why not make the most
Of what the day has to offer
Of what the mind might proffer

BBB Poem 54

Beside the seaside
Throwing pebbles off the beach
A perfect sea
Or at least so I am told
By an oldish lady
Throwing pebbles at a tin can

The quiet then snapped
By the seventh wave landing
With a reasonably ubiquitous crash

Beside the seaside
Squashing pebbles into our bottoms
A vast sea
Or at least I do believe so
With a one hundred and sixty
Degree horizon

The delineation marked
By the last green line of darkness
And the first sky blue of sky

BBB Poem 55

Mushroom, and tarragon soup
Christopher what's come over you
Is it the Suffolk sea air
That is getting near to your inner truth

On the pier at Southwold
Above the waving waves
That travel from the Nuclear power station
To way beyond the newly built sea defences

All pretence of summer is indefensible
Under the grey-black, black-grey skies
All thoughts of English holidays reprehensible
For teenagers who share their lover's cries

BBB Poem 56

The real day zero

There is nothing that I haven't written
Nothing that I have left unsaid
In this place of the last lines
Where the departure words are read

Long coats, smart blazers, and medals
Car parks, and overflow car parks
Roads laid out in the geometric style
For the cortège and the heralds

Say goodbye, and drive away, or fly
Off to the new life; beyond, yes beyond
The flags, and the platoons, the leader
Of the band in his striped tie

A military man, an Air Force man
All grey, and crimson, and royal blue
Laughter, and bonhomie, and o what's new
This is the real day zero, and for today we stand

BBB Poem 57

The concrete and the clay
Beneath my feet begin to crumble
As I stumbled upon a few home truths

The blank page is a blank day
What better way to start anew
When the view is solely of your own making

Step out into the hat ounce of fresh inspiration
With a smile, with a way deeper breath
Recognise that death is only for the dying

Fix your ills, shape your mind, and body
Take time to be anybody, in this world
Where your soul may swirl, dip as the swallow

BBB Poem 58

That one man
With top hat and stick
What does he think of
As he walks before the hearse
Up the hill to the graveside
If he, as they
Could think of pipes and bands
Joy, on this sunshine day of celebration
And now
As the coffin is lifted from he hearse
To be borne on six men's shoulders
Before being carried down the hill
Towards the graveside patrons
Before being lowered
Down into the grave
The recordings of this
His last scene
Are absent
No photographs, no video
No sounds recorded for future playback
Only solemn memories
Of grey skies
And solemn occasions
Thank heavens for the flowers
And the gaily coloured youths

BBB Poem 59

The next lot are due
In this well oiled procession
Of folk who have made enough of life
To be worthy of cremation, or burial

It seems to me, though I am no expert
That a graveside affair offers more opportunity
To unhurried contemplation, also to be able
To think of life in the natural cycle of nature

But it is cold outside, even in September
With frosted words; written, read, and spoken
Whereas the crematorium, as you might expect
Is fairly well heated; but warmer words, no

So there you have it
You take your choice, and you get on with it
Spacious cold comfort farm, or packed tight
On uncomfortable, utilitarian, wooden chairs

BBB Poem 60

Black is the colour of the day
Black is the colour of mourning
Slow is the long walk of the day
Slow is the certainty now dormant

Severe, and serene, and in between
The sounds of walking sticks and shuffled feet
Seek out, whatever it is you must seek out
Among these mild, and meek ways, to torment

BBB Poem 61

I sit still, and look out of the window
I see the settled stillness of nature
Flowers, and bushes, and trees, and sky
I see layers, and layers
Layers of variegated colours
Yellows, and oranges, and reds, and crimsons
Greys, and greens, and blues, and golds
I see all of this
As I watch a television arts programme
About *Still Life*
And I remember my own book
Branch Lines To The Silent
I recall its passage
To it becoming a physical object

I see the settled stillness of nature
And I remember a night of erotic passion
With the vicars daughter
I am reading Doctor Zhivago
I could be the renegade apprentice
I could be the striking railroad worker
I was in those episodes
I did those kinds of things
I lived that life, a little bit out of control
It was the wildness
The wildness before the stillness

I gently unbuttoned
Her see-through blouse, caressed
Her delightful, if somewhat diminutive, breasts
She showed me

How to lubricate a *Durex* gossamer
We made love
Leaning against, and looking into
Into the open castle window
We made love again, down in the town
Behind the gasometer
In earshot of the dancehall
The flowers, the bushes, the trees
And the sky, all still
I saw layers, and layers
Layers of variegated colours
Purples, and pinks, and rouges, and violets
Whites, and silvers, and rubies, and vermilions

BBB Poem 62

I smell the lavender
In the heal repair balm
As I massage after bathing
My mind instantly springs
To you know who
With no call at all
For those way slower
Neural thought processes

I run my fingers over
The roll of decorators lining paper
On the dining table
My mind instantly springs
To my draughtsmanship days
With just a shadow of a sidestep
To the girl, or young woman
In the printing department

BBB Poem 63

Escape to pure indulgence
Awake to a fresh frame of mind
Certain of the uncertainties
Sure of the insecurities

The clearer the put down
The more conscious the response
The calmer the attempt at closure
The more ferocious ones reaction

And with those few words
The here, and the now, becomes forever
Yet, with no lack of quaint absurdity
The past, and the future, are drawn together

What I am looking for at this time
Is something way more impenetrable
Say like a fortress castle wall
Ten feet thick and then some

Then, with the safety of pure resilience
To stake a claim to become ruthless
Pertain to a clearer opportunity
Shaming, shaking your impunity

Hard knocks, are harder to call
Brick blocks, they build the wall
Close doors, to witness the stroll
Dust on floors, ask cameras to roll

BBB Poem 64

I don't have the tears
I don't carry that hollow feeling within me
I don't go out into the night, or out into the day
With the total loss of loss for companion

Instead I have an understanding
I have reconciled myself to the facts
Yes I do still occasionally indulge sadness
But twelve years down the line life is easier

Of course the writing helps; it is healing
It is cathartic, it is therapeutic
And yes, I have to tell you, I must tell you
That just now and then, it stops me in my tracks

Sends me off in the search of past times
(For I know there to be no future)
All of my life being lived again
In no more than a few remembered moments

I don't have the tears
But see you can't help yours
I feel for your desperation
Your hollowed out core

I see that you want to wander
Wilful into the night
Carrying the unbearable weight
Of your loss with you

I have only a sideline understanding

I do try to tease out a few facts, words such
That I might pin on some assistance
To propel you, re-energised, into the turmoil

BBB Poem 65

Love, at its worst
In your tear stained, tear filled eyes
In your wavering, quivering small voice
In your entire abandonment of hope

Love, which had tore into you
Without disguise, or mask
Without certainty, or promise
Without regard for pain

And now here you are
With you love being unrequited
With barriers drawn, yet
With doors left ever so slight ajar

Daring you to repeat yourself
Encouraging you to repeat the performance
In this way he shows his weakness
In this way he shows his love, at its worst

BBB Poem 66

It does not take a lot
To remind me of my stealthy departure
Leaving you for the last time
I drove for fifteen minutes
Through the early morning frosted sunlight
To park up, beside the black water pool
High on Dartmoor's random terrain

That thought in turn takes me back
To that very same, isolated moorland road
On a snow filled night around Christmas
A reckless decision
To make such a dangerous journey
Where all ahead was a works party, without you

I ask for a replacement cup of coffee
The original was neither black, nor strong
In truth the second cup was little better
A connoisseur may tell you
That the coffee was burnt
I trail off, with those unsure, indecisive words
I hope you might see
This poem is no longer for you, or about you

BBB Poem 67

A market town in Lincolnshire

A cash machine with parking spaces

Mon, Tues, Thurs, 30 Mins No return in 30 Mins

The lady, in the estate car

Straddles two bays, such is her rush

Then, after visiting the bank

She moves her car forwards a couple of feet

A small girl, possibly the drivers daughter

Wears a sky-blue ribbon in her hair

They walk off, across the square

I wonder if I shouldn't time them

With a sort of sense of civic duty

BBB Poem 68

So this is where we're at
We've done the this and that
Meddled with the tit for tat
Behaved like the drowning rat

So this is how we are
We pushed ourselves too far
We stopped looking for the star
And drove West in the motor car

Would that October
Could be any other time
Would that to stay sober
Could twist me down the line

Would that February
Was also less weight
Would that to be merry
Could open the gate

But this is where we're at
We missed out on getting back
Settled for defence, or attack
Behaviour of the downright prat

But this is how we are
We raised too high the bar
Stopped smelling molten tar
Drove East in the motor car

BBB Poem 69

The walls are solid
The windows are deeply inset
I am up at four in the morning
Basking in the house apparatus light

Outside, the old stable walls
Are not so strong
And the Virginia Creeper
Why, as it must, it is creeping

BBB Poem 70

Of course I like poetry
Don't I subscribe to the societies
Quarterly magazine
Yes know they are often left unopened
On the sideboard with the post

And don't I every month
Buy a book of new poetry
Or a book of poetry new to me
But no I am sorry
I cannot tell you the name of the last one

Yes I do write other poet's poems
Into my hard-backed notebook
I write in different coloured inks
I write them out for safe keeping
For closer reading
Though there haven't been entries
Not for a while

I have run creative writing & poetry workshops
For over a decade now
Albeit they are for dwindling numbers
Having given up the vigour
Of the spoken word

I enjoy listening to poets on the radio
And watching poetry, in its many guises
On the television, but I wonder
Why is it always the same old faces
And just how old is John Cooper Clarke

Ten years ago, after completing my MA
I asked if I could do a PhD in video poetry
My tutor refused my request
He said it was not a serious subject
I hope he retired, yes, I hope that is the case

I have my own blog, hosted by Blogger
A new poem of mine is posted everyday
With no explanation or background
Yes I know there is a link to buy the pamphlet
But I'm not sure it works, for no one ever has

There is an interview
With me pontificating, questioned
By my partner Kate
Search *coastmoor* on YouTube
It's getting on, but mostly I still feel the same

I never did care
For those intellectuals who deconstruct
And reconstruct at will, their will
Yes Ruth, I am talking about you

Why do I write this
And what is the use of poetry
Well
Today I will judge a poetry competition
So I thought you ought to have my credentials

My votes will be for feelings
Emotions
Inspirations

Creativity, and love: o yes, I must sense love

BBB Poem 71

We have all suffered, she said
I won't do that I again, but I did
Of course I don't imagine
That they would have

Is there a tipping point
The first anorak, or cagoule
The first Harris Tweed
The time to stop playing pool

As a one time mathematician
Could I draw a graph
Take out the photo album
To see when I no longer laugh

Yet this place is all about those
Little spots, of a polite sign
The mushroom soup is off, no bother
A small laugh, Broccoli and Stilton's fine

BBB Poem 72

Leaving, on a Sunday morning
Leaving on a jet plane
Receiving love, on a Sunday morning
Leaving is no way the same

Disbelief, good times come and go
Streams of vapour trails
Belief my love, good times come and go
Streams set out to different sails

BBB Poem 73

I have my own darkness
My dark soul of the night
I have my own pain
Physical, emotional

I follow the dawn light
Welcome my soul to the morning
I have my own pain
In the present, from the past

BBB Poem 74

Awake with the ache, the pure echo
Of the plain pain of torn fibre
Every night becomes the same
The joy of sleep is lost to the insane

Awake with Athens ache, the purest echo
Of yesterday's walk deep among the tissue
As daylight entered, as dusk the same
The coy boys lover has given up the game

BBB Poem 75

Stream, river, pool, pond, puddle, lake, tarn
Water, water and rock, water, rock and culvert
And young men
Young men climbing freestyle
Through the rocky water
Meanwhile, in this huge, open-topped cavern
The mobile telephone
Allows the humanist celebrant
To take a booking
For a funeral
The week after next

BBB Poem 76

Step by step by step by step
I can hear the water now
Let the victories be on parade
I can see the rockfall now

Step by step by step by step
I can feel the glory now
Let the semaphores say the same
I can see the footfall now

Step by step by step by step
I can touch the morning now
Let the articulate show the way
I can see the snowfall now

BBB Poem 77

I don't know this house at all
Other than I am told
It once was a store for calamine

I don't know the colour on the wall
Other than it was sold
In the county's interior decorator store

I listened in to last night's conversation
If I may be so bold
I was only half-way to the Buddhist view

I heard arguments go to and fro
For and against; warm and cold
I was only half-way with the antagonist

I drink my tea, slow and sure
Looking out of the window
A clearer day; more light ahead

I drink my tea as I write these words
Thinking of walks on which to go
A calm for now, a future to second-guess

BBB Poem 78

Autumn sun
Light which I don't recall seeing before
Pink orange in the sky
Highlight light orange on the carpet

And in between
Those ninety three million miles
How many faces to smile upon

Autumnal sky
As yesterday you caught me
Looking through the farmhouse window
For the moment of peak experience

And in between
Those hundred miles or so
From one county to another

Autumn night
A darkness which I am not used to
Flashlights and tall shadows
Adults as children at play

And in between
The public house and the private house
The joviality is continued

BBB Poem 79

Autumn light
EmergingFirst And Last Of Love
From a mist covered pink-red sun

They said
This is how the world will end
With such violent winds, such visceral skies

And so you sit, sit and watch, sit
And listen to the whistle, sit
And listen, listen to the shaking timbers

And so I sit and write, I sit
And write some more, I sit
Until I hear someone knocking at the door

BBB Poem 80

Watch the leaves on the trees
What better to do
Watch grey skies increase
Away from the blue

Watch lover's words permeate
What better to do
Watch hope slowly decrease
Away from the you

Watch the afternoon move on
What better to do
Watch war turn to peace
Away from the new

BBB Poem 81

In the hours
Before the morning light
With time alone
To fall and rise

With time alone
And darkness there
To settle back
Except for pain
Free to stare

Half awake now
With the tea
I share my thoughts
My hopes for me

The certainty
The sanctuary
The beauty
The love

I splashed in rivers
I walked in parks
I climbed mountains
I'm up for the larks

My mind does wander
That much is true
Nostalgia and reverie
To remember but the few

And the many
Who have joined this faith
Not always, or forever
Yet for the meanwhile
We carried the staff

Lived many ways
With tears and smiles
Before the day
And the hours of miles

BBB Poem 82

Where is the frustration
Where is the loss
What makes the dreams
Which sources to emboss

In hope is their certain despair
Being alone are we bound to share
With the past is the present
Pour the ladle in effortless pairs

Rides at the fairground
Drinks in the bar
Sad nights at football
Pushing for a step too far

Turning to faith
With an explorers mind
There for the joy of examination
And the diamonds to find

To swirl as in orbit
Or simply to sit and stare
To meditate on peace
And silently be there

With the hope of a song
As beauty walks by
To know of a truth
By having known the lie

Where is the reality

And where is the fake
Here with my own faith
To riddle, to rake

BBB Poem 83

It's five-thirty-seven
And the shoulder is sore
I view pictures of brethren
And read words for the shore

Those sands which I walked on
As the sun was to rise
Those steady foot settlements
To feel love, love in those eyes

The door is open
The curtains are drawn
Autumn is the season
And the leaves are shorn

I didn't mean to reason
I didn't mean to fawn
I just made mistakes
On the day of the dawn

Like a wheel that turns
With direction unknown
Begging for forgiveness
As you carry the thorn

Nipping, and nattering
And callously borne
Shifting, and shattering
The truth in her eyes

Hoping, yer clattering

So close to despise
Helplessly flattered
By your half-way disguise

BBB Poem 84

I take myself off
To places I've never been
I read of our song
So what does it mean

At six in he morning
Already three times awake
Pretty pictures rolling
I think of River Erne intake

From where water was drawn
But at what cost
Where the puppet was played
While the true love was lost

BBB Poem 85

I reach out to nowhere
Not knowing what to touch
I collect scraps and tit-bits
Yet squander so much

I wave a hand at the dark
Not knowing the friend
I undo words, letters also
I undo, to hold back at the end

I am no different
To millions, zillions of men
All who suffered heartbreak
And now gravitate to zen

BBB Poem 86

I have been unable
To cure myself
Of this long held obsession

I have tried, believe me
Yet every time I throw
Another stone into the water

I smile to myself, politely
I watch the ripples
Dappled and stipples with light

In the deep of night
Her memory is falling
From the moon and stars

As I lay in my bed
I spin the words to thread
The lost love which is calling

Without pad or pen or pencil
I repeat the words
Hoping that my sleep

Will not take them away
But of course it does
So frail is my obsessed mind

BBB Poem 87

Words which enter of their own volition

They are the best words

Just as the glimpse

From the corner of ones eye

Says all that needs to be said about her beauty

Just as the gathering in

Of the one unique scent note

Says all that you need to know about her style

BBB Poem 88

Did we desert each other
Without support structures in place
Did we carry away the voice
Which only knew obstruction, and angst

Did we flunk it as passionately
As first we had made it
Did we put distance, yet more distance
Between us, also behind us

How surly, and insensitive was I
How rigidly representative were you
With love unknown to the logic
Was our rationale simply too too true

BBB Poem 89

It is Nineteen-eighty-seven
I am thirty-five years old
I am stood
Looking out of the window
In the small back bedroom
Of our fairly new detached house

I have a devoted family
Two beautiful children
A good job
A brand new car
My studies are going well
But something isn't right

The black mist has descended
I am frustrated
I want to extend the house
But don't know why, or how
I want to do more with work
But aren't sure what, or how

We have small back garden
Bordered by trees
Conifers and poplars
Which I had planted
One sodden wet
Easter weekend

There is a small, straight
Water-feature, by the patio
To be honest there isn't room

For an extension
I write a poem
It could be the first I ever wrote

It is dark
It is despondent
It is without hope
It cries of my frustrations
It talks of loss
It talks of despair

It is Two-thousand-and-five
I am eighteen years older
I am leaving another house
With a small, straight
Water feature; a rill
As I now name it

It is Two-thousand-and-seventeen
I am looking back
I don't know why, or how
Both water-features are filled in
Both houses have been sold
And sold at least once again

BBB Poem 90

I wrote out a poem
From Lang Leav's book
The Universe Of Us
It wasn't for your birthday
Not as such, for I wrote it out
A few days ago, but then today
I saw another of Lang's poems
On my *Tumblr* web site
And of course today
Today it is your birthday

BBB Poem 91

Several months
Almost a year
Of debilitating pain
Which, however optimistic
One may be superficially
The doubt still remains
The question remains
Will I be cured
Will I be made better

Such the the sleep
Will itself be longer
Than the two hour snatches
Such that the sitting
And the stride about walking
Will be without recourse
To a massage of the shoulder
Or without the need
To nudge a little to the right

I notice the margin is sloping
Yet this is no love poem
No story of abject loss, or lust
For that matter neither a tome
To express the slain of heartbreak
Or the overdue longing of the unrequited
No, not so, however much
I might write of the frozen shoulder
It will always nag away at me

BBB Poem 92

How good do you look
Such that your boyfriend
(I guess he is your boyfriend)
Wants to stop
And take a photograph
Of your shadow
On the cathedral floor

He shows you the shot
And after a few words
You throw your arms around him
And kiss him fully on the lips
Yes, I am pretty sure
He is your boyfriend
At least now I hope so

Ok I know it is not spiritual
Although I do believe love played a part
And I know that is short on religion
Even with the audacious use of the c word

Now it is the thirty-somethings kissing
With their loving teenage children
Trying also to get in on the act
Meanwhile the Breton man
Fondles the stone
And the push chair
Is pushed, and spun, and twirled
The tall man looks up
At the way taller ceiling
And explains to all who are in earshot

The purpose of the arches

BBB Poem 93

I am sat on Joy Ibsen's chair
I don't know if she had much joy in her life
Or if her demeanour lived up to her name
But I guess
As hers is the only name on the chair
She was not lucky
In how might we say, bodily love
Maybe she saved herself
For the good of the lord

Of course I may be mistaken
There may have been more than one suitor
Too many names
To be carved into the elegant chair
Of course it may have been elegance
Elegance above all else
That joy wished to portray
That she wished to be known for
And for many, perhaps
Elegance is next to godliness

BBB Poem 94

Sunday doesn't seem a good day anymore
To delve into the peace and the tranquility
Of there being a deeper purpose to life

Instead it appears to have become a day
For movement, for explorations, for visitors
To arrive from Italy, and France, and Spain

Here to pay their religious respects, of sorts
But also to take numinous photographs
And to explain, to those in earshot

The history, the history of the building that is
Not their history, nor my history, such as it is
No, that life history is left for others to discover

BBB Poem 95

The Clematis Flowers
In late October
After the savage pruning
In the summer

It is as if a soldier
Injured in battle
Had, once recovered
Returned to the front

Now he, and the Clematis
May smile upon the world
To give hope to the rest
That the fight is worthy

BBB Poem 96

Is there some purpose
That you always post
Photographs of you
On your own
Always it seems alone
Not with another

Is there some reason
That I only ever see
Your photographs
With you alone, never
In a loving embrace
With someone other

BBB Poem 97

Does it matter
Where the inspiration comes from
Just so long as the inspiration turns up

Richard Rohr in his book *Immortal Diamond*
Says that *The contemplative mind should be*
religion's unique gift to society. It greases the
wheels of spiritual evolution.

I would rather
That he had not tried to claim this gift
Solely on behalf of religion, for it is my belief that
mankind alone has gifted that beauty, which is the
contemplative mind

And from where that contemplation comes
And to where the contemplation takes me
Is a response entirely down to my own life:
To my highs and lows
My hopes and expectations
To the life I have lived, and which am still living
To my night-time dreams
And to my daily disappointments

I am almost overloaded with the words
And the images from the social media *Tumblr*
Yet I feel good, I feel upbeat, and positive
For having trawled the familiar, and the new
I am pleased
To have had a conversation with my soul
With my friends

Out there in the contemplative ether

BBB Poem 98

There is missing and there is missing
There is longing and there is longing
There is loss and there is loss
There is bright light in abundance
And there is hope
Yes, always there is hope

There is doubt
Doubt and the depth of deep delusion
There is also a music
A music which for some does not sing
There is all of this, in one singular lifetime
But I ask you to believe me
There is hope, there is always hope

There is the sacred
And there is the purple tint profane
There is the blinding truth
And then there is the other game
There is the obtuse, and the downright barmy
But there is hope
And hope lives on, lives on in your name

There is hard work
And there are easier pickings
Some days they may seem to be the same
The toil of honest labour
Or the rolling of the winning dice
For there is hope
And hope is so so happy that you came

There is breath
And there is contemplative breathing
There is meditation
Instead of going to the football
There is a nearness
And a further distance still to fall
But there is hope
Hope which asks that you make the call

There is skin
And there is fabric
And there is skin
There are the living
And the heavenly ethereal bodies
There are shrouded myths
And the legends of the soul
There is hope
Hope which asks that you make the call

Printed in Great Britain
by Amazon

23355915R00078